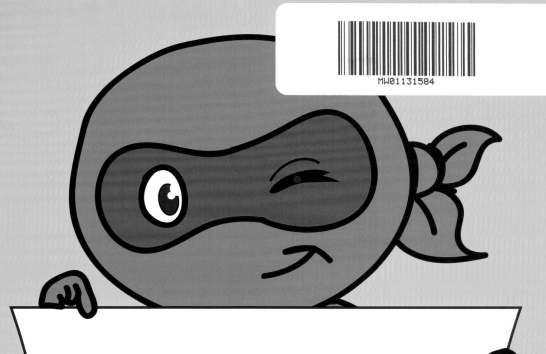

This book belongs to

_____

But Curious Ninja didn't like that very much.

So, I went to find Memory Ninja who was painting a picture of a big tree that grew at the end of the yard.

Memory Ninja looked at me, sighed, and then packed away the paints.

Then, I saw Forgetful Ninja in a tree.

First, I apologized to Curious Ninja who couldn't wait to show me the new game. But then soon Curious Ninja got frustrated while explaining some of the steps of the game. That's when I offered my support...

Next, I stopped by Memory Ninja's place.

For my last stop, I returned to Forgetful Ninja's place.

Building the chairs and ladder were much harder than we both expected. We found ourselves getting frustrated.

Even though we got discouraged at times, we never gave up and continued to support each other.

And it was!

Remembering to build others up could be your secret weapon in building your supportive superpower!